# PYTHON PROGRAMMING FOR BEGINNERS

The Complete Guide for Total Beginner to Learn Python Programming in 1 week.

By

Robert Campbell

# Table of Contents

# Introduction

Programming is becoming an increasingly demanded skill for anything from web design to Machine Learning and the Internet of Things.

It's on its way to having a daily use due to the importance of technology.

While programming used to be a subject that people started studying for their computer science degree, now it is often taught starting from elementary school.

One of the main reasons for its widespread use is accessibility.

You don't need much to get started.

Thanks to the power of the Internet, all you need is a computer and a number of software tools that you can download and install without spending a penny.

In addition, there are many resources to learn from, as well as organized communities you can join and learn from.

You are going to learn why Python is one of the best programming languages to start with, as well as progress your career if this isn't your first language.

Furthermore, you will explore the tools you need, install them, and start your journey.

This will guide you step by step and show you everything you need to know in order to get started.

If you are already familiar with any other programming language such as C, C++, or Java, you might want to skip this or simply glance through it to refresh your memory.

We can define programming as the process of designing, coding, debugging, and maintaining the source code of a computer program, which means that we say the steps to follow for the creation of the source code of computer programs.

The programming language, are all those rules or regulations, symbols, and particular words used for the creation of a program, and with it, offer a solution to a particular problem.

The best-known programming languages are: Basic (1964), C++ (1983), Python (1991), Java (1995), C# (2000), among others.

Programming is one of the stages for software development; programming specifies the structure and behavior of a program, verifying if it is working properly or not.

Programming includes the specification of the algorithm defined as the sequence of steps and operations that the program must perform to solve a problem, for the algorithm to work, the program must be implemented in a compatible and correct language.

We could consider programming even easier than learning a new language because the programming language will be governed by a set of rules, which are, generally, always similar, so you could say that it might be considered as a natural language.

In order to better understand the subject of programming, we could start with the beginnings of programming and how all this universe of languages and programs we know today began.

We could start saying that programming began when the first computer was created in the fifteenth century, when a machine capable of doing basic operations and square roots appeared (Gottfried Wilhelm von Leibniz), although the one that actually served as a great influence for the creation of the first computer was the differential machine for calculating polynomials with the support of Lady Ada Countess (1815-1852), known as the first person who entered programming, and from whom comes the name of the programming language ADA, created by the DoD (Department of the United States), in the 1970s.

# Python - The First Impressions

## What Is Python and Why Is It a Good Programming Language to Learn?

As a beginner who has never done anything with coding, Python is one of the best coding languages to work. Python has long been considered a beginner's language because it is so easy to learn, and you will be able to understand it right from the beginning. This is just one of the many reasons why you should choose to work with Python. You will also like there is a large active community devoted to this programming language and what's good is that it's open source so you can get started without literally having to pay anything. This language will also work on any operating system, so it won't matter which computer you want to use the language on.

Despite being the coding language that beginners like to work with, this doesn't mean that there aren't a lot of advantages that come with working with this language. Python on its own is capable of writing great codes in the process, and you can also combine it with a few other languages so that you can create as many strings of code that you like. Now, let's take some time to look at Python and all the things that you need to know to get started on using this coding language.

## Why should I learn Python?

As we mentioned before, there are a lot of different coding languages that you can learn about and use. So, if there are a lot of choices out there, why would you want to go with the Python coding language in the first place? Many people, both experts, and beginners all choose to go with

Python because it is easy to learn, easy to read, and it is capable of creating large, challenging codes that you might want to write. There are a lot of different reasons that you would want to work with this coding language, and these include:

- Simple enough to read

You will find that Python is a programming language that is very easy to read, even if you are a beginner. When it is compared to some of the other coding languages, it is one of the most readable languages. Since this is a natural coding language to go with, many beginners like that they can catch on so quickly and that they will understand what they are doing in no time.

- Free

Another benefit of going with Python is that it is free to use. There are some computer coding languages that you would have to pay for so you can use them and this can be quite expensive, especially if you want to learn how to use more than one of them. Python is free to use, so you don't have to worry about this problem.

- Fast

Even though this language is natural enough for any beginner to learn, Python is still considered one of the high-level languages that you can learn. This means that when you make a program and generate your codes by using Python, you will see that the execution is friendly and quick. Some coding languages are harder to work with or can't go as fast as you want them to, but this is a problem you won't have when using Python.

- Works on a variety of platforms

You can work with the Python language no matter which platform you would like to use it on. Linux is the operating system that a lot of people will choose to go with, but you can still work with Python even if you are on a Windows or Mac computer. This is excellent news because it means that you can use Python without having to make any significant changes to your current setup.

- A big library to work with

Once you start to get familiar with Python, you will notice that it comes with an extensive library. This is good news for beginners because the library is what contains all the functions, codes and other things that you need to make the language work for you. This library will help make sure that you can do some useful stuff when trying to make your code.

- A large community

Whether you have worked with coding language in the past or not, it is nice to know that there is a large community of Python users that will help you out if you ever get stuck. Any time that you need some ideas like a new project or if you have a question, or if you want to learn something new, there is a library of information to provide you with the information that you need to help you get started.

## How Python Works

You know a handful of terms related to python, so let's take a step back for a second and talk about what makes python the way it is. It is an "object-oriented" programming language. To understand this, you should first know what functions are. Also known as subroutines or procedures, functions manipulate data and allow you to use code multiple times in a program without copying the code over and over again. Functions are front-and-centre when using a procedureoriented style of programming, but it doesn't always work very well when you're writing more extensive programs. That's when objectoriented programming becomes more useful. Python does not prioritize functions, but it still uses them.

Objects and classes When you combine data and function, you get an object. The Python Programiz website describes objects as a collection of data (variables) and function. In the real world, a car or house is an object. Just like every object needs a design or blueprint, every object in Python needs a class, and like design plans, classes contain all the information and details needed to create the object. That process of creation is called instantiation (which begins whenever you type in the keyword class) while the resulting object is known as an instance of a class. You use classes when you need to keep data related to each other organized and grouped.

## Attributes and methods

Classes need functionality attached to them, or what's the point? You achieve functionality by setting attributes, which hold the data related to functions, which in Python are known as methods. Confused? Let's look at the example HackerEarth uses:

class Snake:

name: "diamondhead"

You just created a new class, Snake, and assigned the word "name" to the word "diamondhead." That makes sense visually. Whenever you want to refer back to this information, you want the program to know that the snake name is diamondhead. The class needs to be assigned to a variable, like so:

```
snake = Snake()
```

Now, you can retrieve the attribute, which in this case is diamondhead. We should first explain the dot notation, which is a literal dot or period. Using this tells Python to look inside the space that is before the dot. Whatever is inside the space is the code that Python should execute.

You would type in:

```
print(snake.name)
```

You just told Python to look at Snake, which leads it back to Snake (), which leads it back to the class you created. When you run this program, you end up with:

```
print(snake.name)
```

diamondhead That's the essence of classes and methods. Methods are always associated with a class.

Inheritance Before moving on from classes, let's explore what inheritance means. This is the processing of reusing code, which is one of the benefits of object-oriented programming. Let's say you're continuing work on your snake project, and you want to organize the reptile into two types: water snakes and land snakes. You know that they share some characteristics, such as being legless and having flicky tongues, but there are also specific characteristics associated with the different snakes. Now, you could create two separate classes, but adding a new common characteristic would mean you have to add it into both of them, and that can quickly become annoying.

What you want to do instead is use the inheritance mechanism. You are creating a type and subtype connection between your classes. Create one class that both water and land snakes can pull - or inherit from. Your water and land snakes become sub-types, so when you add your standard features (legless, flicky tongues) to just that parent class, they show up in both sub-types. You are free to add unique and separate features into the sub-types.

Inheritance makes it way easier to keep things organized and to reuse code. You have this base or parent class that sets everything up, and if you need to modify just a piece of it or use its essential functions with some changes, you can refer back to it while creating a new subtype, and then add (to the sub-type) without messing up the parent class.

Loops Using loops can also help reduce the amount of code you have to write out every time you want the program to achieve something. Looping is not exclusive to Python; it can be employed in just about every computer language. A loop is a sequence of instructions that keep repeating within the perimeters you set up until the condition you establish is met. It allows you to execute statements or entire groups of comments multiple times without writing out the code each time.

There are two main types of loops in Python: for loops and while loops. For loops run a predetermined number of times, no matter what..

While loops will repeat a single statement or group while the given condition is correct, there is no predetermined number of times for this loop; it's all about true or false. Before beginning the loop, Python tests the condition to confirm whether or not it is true. It will keep executing a block while the state is true, and it will stop if it becomes false.

It is even possible to "nest" a loop, so you're getting a loop within the loop, or an inner loop and an outer loop. Python will cycle through the outer loop, and when it's made a full pass, it triggers the inner loop, which in turn triggers the outer loop again once its run is complete.

You can stop any type of loop by writing break and even skip over a part of code and then begin the loop again by writing continue. Why would you do this? It's advantageous if there are only certain parts of a code you want to use again. Without the option of breaking and continuing the loop, you would have to copy the entire code and then delete the part(s) you didn't want. It's much cleaner to loop. You would usually put your break and continue statement after a certain condition is met. How do you tell Python to be aware of that? You use a conditional if statement.

Conditional statements Pretty much all programming languages make use of an if statement, which is the main type of conditional statement. It is an essential part of Python's ability to make decisions about running code or not, and if necessary, change a program's flow. The if the statement is similar to a while loop in that it only runs if certain conditions are met, but unlike a while loop, conditionals only run once. Loops make use of conditional statements, but conditional statements do not require loops.

So, you tell Python you want a bit of code only if something is true. To test that, Python uses a Boolean expression, which is just a fancy way of describing a statement that is either true or false. If the answer ends up being false - the conditions are not met - what then? You will use else or elif statements. An else statement just tells the computer what the next step should be, like what block of code it should skip to instead of running the original which doesn't meet the conditions you want.

# Getting ready for Python

You can run and code Python on Windows, Mac, and Linux. To get started, head over to the official website: www.python.org and download the Python installer. This book will use Windows as the primary environment for the examples and lessons.

## Python 2.x vs. Python 3.x

There are two popular and official versions of Python: Python 3.x and 2.x. As of this writing, you can download Python 3.7.0 if you want the 3.x version. You can also download Python 2.7.15 if you want the 2.x version.

However, to prevent any conflicts and misunderstandings, please download and use Python 3.x. All the examples and lessons in this book are written with Python 3.x in mind.

The 2.x version is an older version of Python. Ever since the Python developers proceeded in developing Python 3.x, they have made a lot of changes to the behavior and even the syntax of the Python programming languages.

For example, if you divide 3 and 2 using the '/' operator in Python 2.x, you will receive an output of 1. If you divide the same numbers with the same operator in Python 3.x, you will receive an output of 1.5.

You may ask: If Python 3.x is new and improved, why are the developers keeping the old versions and why is Python 2.x being used?

The quick answer to that is code migration. Because there are many differences between version 2.x and version 3.x, programs and scripts created using version 2.x need to be recoded to become compatible with version 3.x Python.

If you are dealing with a small program using version 2.x, then the code migration will be a trivial problem at best. However, if you have programs with thousands of lines, then migration can become a huge problem. Other issues with migrating to Python 3.x are code maintenance and retraining programmers to adapt with the changes.

Because of the aforementioned reasons, developers with huge programs written and ran using the version 2.x runtime environment did not bother making the transition to version 3.x.

## Installing the Interpreter

Python comes with two important 'programs': Python's runtime environment and command line interpreter. The Python installer you download from its website contains both. Installing them is easy, particularly in Windows.

All you need to do is download the file and click open to let it run the setup. You will need to follow a few simple step-by-step instructions, click a few buttons here and there and Python will be available on your computer.

Note that there will be a point during the installation that you will need to select the packages and features that you want to be installed in your system. Make sure that you check all of them.

Note that tcl/tk installs TkInter, which is a Graphic User Interface (GUI) toolkit you need if you plan to create windows for your programs. The Integrated Development and Learning Environment (IDLE) require and depend on TkInter since it is a Python program with a GUI.

Also, for now, check the Python test suite feature. You will need it later. Finally, PIP is an optional feature that allows you to download Python packages later.

If you believe you do not need some of them, just make sure that the checkbox for IDLE and Python Test Suite are selected.

## Using Python Shell and IDLE

There are two ways to run a Python program. And that is using its runtime environment or using the command line interpreter. The command line interpreter has two forms. The first one is the regular Python shell. The second one is IDLE or Integrated Development and Learning Environment.

The regular Python shell uses the familiar command line interface (CLI) or terminal look while IDLE is a Python program encased in a regular graphical user interface (GUI) window. IDLE is full of easy to access menu, customization options, and GUI functions while the Python shell is devoid of those and only offer a command prompt (i.e. the input field in a text-based user interface screen).

One of the beneficial functions of IDLE is its syntax highlighting. The syntax highlighting function makes it easier for programmers or scripters to identify between keywords, operators, variables, and numeric literals.

Also, you can customize the highlight color and the font properties displayed on IDLE. With the shell, you only get a monospaced font, white font color, and black background.

All of the examples in this book are written in the Python shell. However, it is okay for you to write using IDLE. It is suited for beginners since they do not need to worry about indentation and code management. Not to mention that the syntax highlighting is truly beneficial.

## Writing Your First Program

To get you started, code the below Hello World program. It has been a tradition for new programmers to start their learning with this simple program. Just write this line in the shell or IDLE and press Enter.

```
>>> print("Hello World!")

Hello World!

>>> _
```

## Shell, IDLE, and Scripts Syntax

Programming languages, just like a regular human language like English, have grammar/writing rules or syntax. Syntax rules in programming languages are simple but strict.

Unlike humans, the computer and computer programs like compilers and interpreters cannot understand context. They require precise and proper statements to know what you want. A simple syntax error can stop your program from functioning or make the computer put a stop on your program.

## **Prompt**

The Python Shell and IDLE has a prompt, which looks like this: >>>. You generally start writing your code after the prompt in the Python Shell and IDLE. However, remember that when you write code in a file, py script, or module, you do not need to write the prompt.

For      example:

```
Class thisClass():

    def function1():

        x = 1

        print(x)


    def function2():

        pass
```

That is valid code.

## Indentation

When programming, you will encounter or create code blocks. A code block is a piece of Python program text (or statement) that can be executed as a unit, such as a module, a class definition or a function body. They often end with a colon (:).

By default and by practice, indentation is done with four spaces. You can do away with any number of spaces as long as the code block has a uniform number of spaces before each statement. For example:

```
def function1():

    x = 1

    print(x)
```

```
def function2():

        y = "Sample Text"

        print("Nothing to see here.")
```

That is perfectly valid code. You can also use tab, but it is not recommended since it can be confusing and you will get an error if you mix using tabs and spaces. Also, if you change the number of spaces for every line of code, you will get an error. Here is an example in the shell. Note the large space before print(x) on line 2.

```
>>> x = 1
```

```
>>>      print(x)

 File "<stdin>", line 1

  print(x)

  ^

IndentationError: unexpected indent

>>> _
```

By the way, a statement is a line of code or instruction.

## Indentation Prompt

When using the Python Shell, it will tell you when to indent by using the prompt (...). For example:

```
>>> def function1():

    x = 1

    print(x)


>>> def function2():

    y = "Sample Text"

    print("Nothing to see here.")


>>> _
```

In IDLE, indentation will be automatic. And to escape an indentation or code block, you can just press Enter or go to the next line.

## Python Shell Navigation

You cannot interact using a mouse with the Python Shell. Your mouse will be limited to the window's context menu, window commands such as minimize, maximize, and close, and scrolling.

Also, you can perform marking (selecting), copying, and pasting, but you need to use the windows context menu for that using the mouse. You can also change the appearance of the window and shell by going through the properties menu.

Most of the navigation you can do in the shell is moving the navigation caret (the blinking white underscore). You can move it using the navigation keys (left and right arrow keys, PgUp, PgDn, Home, End, etcetera). The up and down arrow keys' function is to browse through the previous lines you have written.

## IDLE Navigation

The IDLE window is just like a regular GUI window. It contains a menu bar where you can access most of IDLE's functionalities. Also, you can use the mouse directly on IDLE's work area as if you are using a regular word processor.

You might need to take a quick look at the menu bar's function for you to familiarize yourself with them. Unlike the Python shell, IDLE provides a lot more helpful features that can help you with programming.

Primarily, IDLE is the main tool you can use to develop Python programs. However, you are not limited to it. You can use other development environment or word processors to create your scripts.

## Troubleshooting Installation Issues

First of all, make sure that you download the installation file from the website: https://www.python.org. Next, make sure that you chose the proper installation file for your operating system. There are dedicated installation files for Windows, MacOSX, and other UNIX based operating system.

If your computer is running on Windows XP, the latest release of Python will not work on it. You must install and use Python 3.4. Also, remember that there are two versions of each release: a 32-bit and a 64-bit version. If you are unsure if your computer is running on 32 or 64-bit, then just get the 32-bit version. Normally, the recommended installer that the site will provide contains both and will automatically detect which installer it will use.

Normally, you do not need to go to Python's website to download the installation file if you are using a Linux distribution as an operating system. You can just use your system's package manager.

Before installing Python, make sure that you have at least 100 MB free disk space. You can also edit the installation location of Python. However, take note of the location you type it if you wish to install Python in a different folder.

If the installer did not provide shortcuts for you, you can just create them. The Python shell is located in the root folder of your Python installation.

<Python installation folder>\python.exe

For example:

"C:\Python37\python.exe"

For IDLE, you can use its batch file located in

<Python installation folder>\Lib\idlelib\idle.bat

For example:

"C:\Python37\Lib\idlelib\idle.bat"

If you cannot find the idlelib folder inside the Python Lib folder, reinstall Python and make sure that IDLE is checked.

# The world of Variables and Operators

## Variables of Python

Variable is another name for Python identifiers. Variable is a term that is used to imply a memory zone of a machine or device. In Python, you don't need to decide these kinds of factors as Python is a kind of infers programming language and is astute enough to get its variables sort.

Moreover, we may say that the Variables in Python are memory locations, having different data types, such as integers or characters. Variables in Python are just changeable and manipulable because they use a set of various operations.

In any case, variables need a letter or an underscore to get initialized. It is suggested to use lower-case letters as the variable names. In Python, sledge, and Mallet, both are two exceptional elements.

- The naming of Variables or Identifier

Factors are the situations of identifiers. A variable is used to conceive the literal coefficients and the integers used in your program. For Python, the standards to name a variable are given below.

- The essential character of an identifier must be a letter altogether, or an underscore "_".
- Each one of the characters besides the essential characters may be a letter arranged by lower case "a-z," capitals "A-Z," underscores or digits "0-9".
- A variable's name must not contain any void or empty zone, or any special or extraordinary character, such as, "! @, #, %, ^, and, *".

- A variable's name must not resemble any catchphrase portrayed in your Python program's syntax.
- In Python, variables are case sensitive. For example, i'm cool, and I'm cool isn't proportionate.
- Instances of considerable identifiers: n696, _v, v_69, etc.
- Instances of invalid identifiers: 5a, v%69, x69, etc.
- Multiple Assignments

Python enables one to maintain an incentive to various identifiers in an only explanation, which is usually called various assignments. It can be applied in two different ways either by declaring out a solitary incentive for multiple identifiers at the same time or relegating various qualities to numerous variables at different times.

Example - 1:

Open the Python console or IDE and write the command to declare variables.

>>> n=v=w=69

>>> print

>>> print (n, v, w)

Output:

When you type the command to print the value of variables, the output will be something like this.

>>> 69, 69, 69

>>>

Example – 2:

```
>>> n, v, w = 69, 74, 36
>>> print
>>> print (n)
>>> print (v)
>>> print (w)
```

Output:

For output,

When you will type your command

```
>>> print (n)
```

Your console will print "69"

When you will type your command

```
>>> print (v)
```

Your console will print "74"

When you will type your command

```
>>> print (w)
```

Your console will print "36"

## Operators in Python

In general, operators are the language-specific syntactic tokens that require some action to be performed. Operators are mainly derived from the concepts of Mathematics. For example, "Sign of Multiplication (*)" is an operator used in Python programming. It is used to multiply two numbers.

In Python, operators are portrayed as a symbolic representation of a function that does a particular act between two operands to achieve some specific and desired results. Operators are viewed as the mainstays of a program on which your program works in an individual computer programming language. The assortment of operators given by Python is portrayed as pursues. Here are some commonly used operators to perform specific operations:

- Arithmetic Operators
- Comparison Operators
- Assignment Operators
- Logical Operators
- Bitwise Operators
- Membership Operators
- Identity Operators

We are going to discuss some of the above mentioned operators in this part.

- Arithmetic Operators

Arithmetic operators are used to perform particular arithmetic operations to get the desired results. In this case, two operands are taken, and between them, activity through an operator is performed, resulting in some desired, specific, and absolute value.

Here are some of the critical and useful arithmetic operators, which are commonly used in Python.

- Addition "+"
- Subtraction "-"
- Division "/"
- Multiplication "*"
- Remainder "%"

A detailed description of these operators:

- Addition Operator "+"

This operator is used to perform addition or sum function between two operands.

Example:

>>> n, v = 25, 69

>>> n + v

Your console will print "94", in this case.

- Subtraction Operator "+"

This operator is used to take the first operand and subtracts the second operand from the first one.

Example:

>>> n, v = 69, 25

>>> n - v

Your console will print "44", in this case.

- Division Operator "/"

This operand takes the second operand and divides the first operand on the second operand, and gives quotient, as your output.

Example:

>>> n, v = 4, 2

>>> n / v

Your console will print "2.0", in this case.

- Multiplication Operator "*"

As explained earlier, this operator performs the multiplication operation between the first operand and the second.

Example:

>>> n, v = 4, 2

>>> n * v

Your console will print "8", in this case.

- Remainder Operator "%"

This operator is responsible for the operation of division, and it gets the remainder as your output.

Example:

>>> n, v = 4, 2

>>> n % v

Your console will print "0", in this case.

- Comparison operator in Python

Comparison operators, in Python, are used to compare two operands and returns a Boolean type, i.e., TRUE or FALSE, respectively.

- ==

True: This operator is used if and only if the values are logically equal and true.

- !=

True: This operator is used when the values are true but unequal.

- <=

True: This operator is used when the first operand is smaller than or equal to the second operand.

- >=

True: This operator is used when your first operand is greater than or equal to the second operand.

- <>

True: This operator is used if and only if the values are not equal.

- >

True: This operator is used when your first operand is greater than the second operand.

- <

True: This operator is used when your first operand is less than the second one.

- Assignment operators in Python

In Python, we use assignment operators to assign the value to the left operand, of the right-side expression.

- =

Frequently, this operator is used to assign the value of the right expression to the left operand.

- +=

This operator is used to build the estimation of the left operand by the estimation of the correct operand and appoint the altered an incentive back to the left operand.

Example:

>>> n = 2, v = 4

>>> n += v

This will be equivalent to

>>> n = n + v

>>> print (n)

And your console may print the value if n as "6".

- -=

As far as this operator is concerned, it diminishes the estimation of the left operand by the estimation of the correct operand and dole out the changed an incentive back to the left operand.

Example:

>>> n, v = 4, 2

PYTHON FOR BEGINNERS BY ROBERT CAMPBELL

>>> n -= v

This will be equivalent to

n = n - v

>>>print (n)

And your console may print the value if n as "2".

- *=

It increases the estimation of the left operand by the estimation of the correct operand and appoint the altered an incentive back to the left operand.

Example:

>>> n, v = 4 , 2

>>> a * = b

This will be equivalent to

n = n * v

>>> print (n)

And your console may print the value if n as "8".

- %=

This operator is responsible for Divides the estimation of the left operand by that of the correct operand and appoint the update back to the left operand.

Example:

```
>>> n, v = 4 , 2
```

```
>>> a % = b
```

This will be equivalent to

```
n = n % v
```

```
>>> print (n)
```

And your console may print the value if n as "0".

- Logical Operators in Python

As far as our real lives are concerned, sometimes, we have to make tough choices based upon logical data, i.e., true or false. For example, let us say if someone calls you and asks you, "Are you at home?" You would have two choices, "Yes! I am home" or "No! I am not." This would lie under 0 (false) and 1 (true), in programming. This is known as logical data.

In Python, Logical operators are used to evaluate the expressions to obtain some specific decisions. These operators are highly helpful to write any logic reasonably. Here is the list of logical operators with a brief description to build a better understanding with these operators in Python.

Logical Operator Description

- And Operator

If an expression "n" is true, and another expression "m" is true as well, then the result will be true. In any other case, the result will be false.

This table may help you to understand "and operator", in a better way.

| n | v | n and v |
|---|---|---------|

True  True  True

True  False False

False True  False

False False False

- Or Operator

This will result in false, if and only if both operands are false. Consider an expression "n" is true, and another expression "v" is false, then the result will be true.

This table may help you to understand "and operator", in a better way.

n m n or m

T rue T rue T rue

T rue F alseT rue

F alseT rue T rue

F alseF alseF alse

# Data Types

## Python Labels

Before we dive into learning all the data types, let's take a side step and discuss labels. Writing code involves naming variables and objects appropriately so that you can understand what you're looking at immediately. Labels, also known as identifiers, are words represent something in such a way that it makes the code easier to read. For instance, if you're talking about a bottle of water in your code, you shouldn't name the variable that represents it as "var1". That tells you nothing and it makes the entire code confusing. You would have to waste a great deal of time until you figure out which variable you're talking about.

Whenever you name your variables, make sure they are well represented by the label and that they are unique. Do not use the same name multiple times or you will confuse yourself, and worse the program itself. Furthermore, you should avoid similar words as well. We learned earlier how important code commenting is, however, if used in combination with proper identifiers you will not have any problems understanding your code. However, you should take note that certain words cannot be used as labels. These words are exceptions because they are part of Python's own library of keywords that are reserved for various commands. You should read the language's documentation in order to learn which words are reserved, however, some of them are: global, while, False, class, import and so on.

Keep in mind that using an IDE or even certain text editors can help you out with writing proper labels. They can't read your mind, but they will tell you whenever you are trying to use a reserved keyword. This is another advantage of using dedicated programming tools. You won't have to keep a sticky note with all the keywords attached to your monitor.

## Introduction to Variables

In Python, the variable definition is handled in two steps. The first step is called the initialization and it refers to determining the container which is identified via a label. The second step involves the assignment, which means you attach a value to your variable and therefore determine the type of data it holds. These two steps are actually taken at the same time and the process is more of a theoretical one that you don't really notice. Here's how all of this can be formulated:

myVariable = thisValue

The two steps we learned are taken through the equal operator. What we have here is called a statement, in this case an assignment statement. When you write code, you should always keep your statements in proper order. Keep in mind that Python processes code by analysing it from the top to bottom and then it starts over. Furthermore, you could write the statements in the same line, however, that would lead to a lot of chaos.

Now that you know what a variable is, let's see how Python is able to determine which data type is assigned to the variable.

Python has this feature called dynamic typing, which means that it is able to automatically determine what kind of variable it is dealing with. So if you assign an integer to a variable, Python automatically knows that the variable has an integer data type. When working with other programming languages, you have to declare what type of data your variable will contain. Therefore, if it's an integer you have to declare it first and then assign an integer value to it. This is another advantage of working with Python. All you have to do is write your code without worrying too much about the details. Let the interpreter do the heavy lifting for you.

Furthermore, if you make the mistake of performing an operation on a data type that is not eligible for that operation, Python will let you know. However, there is one disadvantage when relying on this system. Because you don't have to declare your variable's data type, as a beginner, you might accidentally create a variable when you don't need one, or assign the wrong data type to it. It's not always easy to pay attention to all the variables you created, however, this problem can easily be fixed.

The best practice when writing a program is to declare all of your variables at the beginning of your project. Keep in mind that the program isn't affected by simple assignments because you aren't instructing the interpreter to perform any operation. If you say x is equal to 10 that's all there is to it. It doesn't really mean anything else. However, by keeping all of your eggs in the same basket you will be able to keep track of them. Keep in mind that this doesn't mean you have to come up with all of your variables from the beginning. You can always return to the start of your program and declare them whenever you need to.

## Strings

The string is the most basic data type, along with numbers. You have actually already used a string when you wrote your first program. The line of text you printed is considered a string. Simply put, strings are sets of characters that are defined between quotation marks. Keep in mind that text also includes numbers and punctuation marks. Even though numbers are normally classified under their own data types such as integers and floats, if you write them between quotes, they are considered textual characters part of a string.

In your first program you had a single statement that was printed with the print function. Keep in mind that you can also print any number of statements, even in the same line, even if they are represented by several variables. This is done with one of the most popular operations you will perform on strings called concatenation. This concept is simple. All it involves is linking multiple strings together. Here's a simple example:

charRace = "human"

charGender = "male"

print (charRace,    charGender)

The output will be "human male".

As you can see, we have two variables and each one of them holds a string. We can print both of them by separating the variables with commas when writing the print statement. Keep in mind that there are multiple ways you can do this. For instance, if you don't want to use variables but you need to concatenate the strings, you can get rid of the commas inside the print statement. You will notice a little problem, though. Here's the example:

print ("school" "teacher")

The result is "schoolteacher". What happened? We didn't leave any whitespace. Take note that whitespace can be part of a string just as numbers and punctuation marks. If you don't leave a space, words will be glued together. The solution is to simply add one blank space before or after one of the strings, inside the quotes.

Next, let's see what happens if you try to combine the two methods and concatenate a variable together with a simple string.

print (charRace "mage")

This is what you will see:

File "<stdin>", line 1

print (characterGender "warrior")

^ SyntaxError: invalid syntax

Congratulations, you got your first syntax error. What's the problem here? We tried to perform the concatenation without using any kind of separator between the two different items.

Let's take a look at one more method frequently used to concatenate a set of strings. Type the following:

x = "orc"

y = " mage"

x + y

As you can see you can apply a mathematical operator when working with string variables. In this case, we add x to y and achieve string concatenation. This is a simple method and works just fine, however, while you should be aware of it, you shouldn't be using it. Mathematical operations require processing power. Therefore, you are telling your Python program to use some of your computer juice on an operation that could be written in such a way as to not consume any resources. Whenever you work on a project, at least a much more complex one, code optimization becomes one of your priorities and that involves managing the system's resource requirement properly. Therefore, if you have to concatenate a large number of string variables, use the other methods that don't involve any math.

## Numbers

Numbers, just like strings, are basic but frequently used no matter how simple or complex your program is. Assigning a number to a variable is done exactly the same as with any other data type. You simply declare it like so:

x = 10

y = 1

Don't forget that Python will automatically know which data type we're assigning. In this case, it identifies our values as integers. Integers are whole numbers that can be either positive or negative. It cannot contain decimal points.

Another numeric data type we mentioned earlier is the float. This is a float:

x = 10.234

Floats can be negative or positive numbers but they must have decimal points, otherwise they're just integers.

Finally, we have the third numeric data type, which is the boolean. This type holds only two values. It can either be true or false, or in computer language 1 or 0. Booleans are normally used together with logical operators instead of mathematical operators like integers and floats.

### Basic Operators

Now that you know a few data types and got used to working with variables, let's start actually performing some handy operations. Variables that hold integers or floats can be manipulated by using the most basic arithmetic operators. For instance, you can subtract, add, multiply, and divide. Whenever you work with these operators you will create an expression instead of a statement. What does that mean? Expressions are essentially code that has to be processed by the computer system in order to find the value. Let's take a look at some exercises you can play with:

apples = 10 + 2

bananas = 10 - 4

pears = 6 * 2

fruit = apples + bananas * pears

fruit

84

Did you perhaps forget your elementary math and expected to see 216 as the result? That's probably because you calculate the sum in your head and then multiplied it. However, that's not how this calculation works. Python automatically knows which rules to follow and it processes each operation in the order it is required.

As you can see, Python is capable of evaluating the expression and then deciding which blocks need to be processed before other blocks. This order that the programming language follows is called an operator precedence. Always pay attention to basic mathematical and logical rules because if you don't, Python will. If you had something else in mind for your program for instance, and you wanted the result to be 216, you need to write the operation to reflect that. In order words, you need to calculate the sum first and then multiply it.

In this example we only worked with integers in order to showcase the most basic operators. However, if you would replace them with floats, the same rules apply.

In addition, it's worth mentioning that Python is capable of converting an integer to a float or even to a string. Any number can be converted to an integer by typing "int (n)", or a float by typing "float (n)" or a string by typing str (objectname).

You'll notice that these are functions because they follow the same structure as the print function which you used earlier. Once we declare the function we want to use, we need to place the value or variable or object in between the parentheses in order to manipulate it. Here's how these basic conversions work:

float (13)

Result: 13.0

int (13.4)

Result: 13

Now that you know the basics, you should start practicing on your own. Create a few different variables and think of all the operations you can perform with them. Don't forget that reading is not enough and you should always take the extra time to practice.

# Making Your Program Interactive

Because you have learned all these preliminaries, it is now the time to start typing some actual code and run them interactively on your python program. Note that you had already started typing in the python interactive session by typing two lines of information text that not only gave the Python version number but also a few hints as illustrated in our early discussion. Usually, the result of our code will be displayed below the input lines when we work interactively and this is after pressing the Enter key. When you type the print statement at the prompt, for example, a Python string also called output will echo back right away. Therefore, there is no need of creating a source code file or run the code a compiler if you are not using Python language. Later, you will learn how to run multiline statements and such statements run as soon as they are entered in their lines and press Enter button twice.

Reasons for the Interactive Prompt

Even though the interactive prompt will echo the results when you run it, it will not save the code in the file. This shows that you cannot handle the bulk of coding in the interactive sessions as you may think. The interactive prompt has turned out to be a good place to test program files or experiment the language on the fly.

Experimenting

Due to its ability to execute the code immediately, the interactive prompt has become the best place to experiment with language. It will be used to illustrate some smaller experiments in this book later. If you are not sure about the working of python code, you can see what takes place when you ire up the interactive command line. If you are reading code in the Python program, for example, you may see an expression that you do not understand its meaning. Example of such expressions could be 'Spam!'*8. You will spend a lot of your time reading the manuals, or books, or even search over the internet to see its meaning.

With immediate response you will receive at the interactive prompt, you can use it to quickly determine the working of the code. From here, for instance, it is clear that code does string repetition. The sign '*' is used in Python to mean the multiplication of numbers as well as repetition for the strings. It is just like concatenating the strings to themselves repeatedly. You will not break anything by this experiment. Generally, Python code is the most appropriate to run as it does not result in the deletion of the files.

Moreover, it is an error to use a variable that has not been assigned value in Python programming. Some errors can go undetected if you fill the names in with defaults. Therefore, to do away with such errors, it is important to start initial counters from zero before adding anything to them and also make sure you have initial lists to help you extend them properly. With initial lists and counting from zero, you will be able to run your program without producing any error

Testing

In addition to serving as a tool or experimenting, the interactive interpreter is used to test the code you will be writing in the files while learning the Python language. In fact, we will show you how to import the module files interactively. Also, we will show you how to run the tests on the tools defined by typing calls at the interactive prompt.

Additionally, many programmers test programming components at the interactive prompt. As a programmer you can import, test, and run functions and classes in the Python files regardless of their sources. This is achieved by typing calls to linked-in-C functions as well as exercising Java classes in Python. Finally, with the interactive nature of the Python, it is able to support an experimental programming style thus making it convenient for you to get started. This is making the Python programming to be simple, easy, and best for beginners to use to run the code on their programs.

Guidelines for using the Interactive Prompt Effectively

Even though it is easy to use interactive prompt, as a beginner, there are many things you should consider when using it to ensure your code runs without producing errors. The following guidelines will help you to avoid making common mistakes seen by other beginners. Just take your time to read them:

- Ensure you only type Python command.

In many cases, beginners make a big mistake by typing system commands in the interactive prompt. This makes their computer to display errors when they try to run their programs. Even though there are many different ways of running system commands from the python code, these methods do not involve typing the commands themselves as you will see in this book.

- Only use print statements in the files

After seeing that interactive interpreter prints the results of an expression automatically, there is no need for you to complete typing print statements in the interactive python. Although interactive interpreter is a nice feature, it sometimes confuses many programmers particularly the beginners when writing code in the files as they must use print statements to make sure that their results are not automatically echoed.

- Avoid indenting at the interactive prompt

Whether you are typing into a text file or interactively, it is important to make sure that all your untested statements start all the way to the left in column 1. In case you don't follow the above instruction, Python will print syntax error since the black space of your code will be taken as indentation for grouping nested statements. Remember that a leading space will always generate an error message if you start with tab or space at the interactive prompt.

- Make sure you note all prompt changes

These changes are essential for compound statements. Although we will not be working with compound /multiline statements at the moment, it is important to know that typing line 2 of a compound statement interactively can make the prompt to change automatically.

- Make sure that the compound statements are terminated at the interactive prompt that has a blank line.

A blank line plays a vital role in Python programming as it tells interactive python a programmer has completed typing the multiline statement and you only need to press the Enter button twice. However, it is not a must to use it in a file. You can ignore them if they are present.

## Entering Multiline Statements

Most of the beginners do not know how to enter multiline statements in the Python program. For instance, last week, we received many emails and messages from the students across the world looking or clarification about entering compound statements. Though it sounds like a hard thing, it is the easiest things to handle with the Python programming languages. To help you understand this, we will introduce compound statements and discuss their syntax in details.

Since they have different behavior or their behavior differs at the interactive prompt and in the file, the following steps are essential for anyone entering multiline statements. Terminate all the compound statements including those for loops and test if there are blank lines at the interactive prompt. Similarly, you can terminate all compound statements before running it by pressing the Enter button twice.

System Command Lines

Even though you can use an interactive prompt to carry out testing and experimenting of your python code, one of the issues associated with it is that your programs disappear immediately they are executed by the Python interpreter. We cannot run the code we have already typed without retyping it since it is not stored in a file. We only need to retype it from scratch or we can cut-and-paste it. However, to carry out this process effectively, we will have to edit out the python prompt and program outputs.

Additionally, we can save our programs permanently by writing our codes in the files, popularly called modules. Modules refer to simple text files that contain python statements. After coding, we will be able to ask the Python interpreter to execute the statement in various ways such as system command lines, file icon clicks, and IDLE user interface. It will execute our code from bottom in a module file every time we run the files. There are many terminologies used in this domain. In Python, for example, module files are called programs. In other words, a program is seen as a series of pre-coded statements in a file executed repeatedly. Sometimes, module files run directly are called scripts, a term that is used to formerly mean a top-level program file in Python. Also, some programmers use the term module to mean a file imported from another file. We will see how these terms are used later in this book.

No matter how you call them, we will explore different ways of running code that are typed into the module files. We will concentrate on the basic ways of running the files. This will involve listing names in a python command line entered at the system prompt o our computer. Although this can be avoided using a GU such as IDLE as we will see later, a system shell and text editor window constitute more integrated development environment, thus providing programmers with direct control over their programs.

First Script

Make sure you have a conducive environment, that is, there is no disturbance before we start working on our first project now. To get started, let us open up our favorite text editor, either the IDLE editor or Notepad and type the following words in the new text file called scrpt1.spy, and then save them in our working code directory that we had set earlier.

Note

We have added some formal Python comments, including text after the #characters. This is necessary in Python as it makes the lines formal by themselves. Also, you should know that the text after # is always seen as a human-readable comment, and as such not considered to be part of the syntax statements. Therefore, there will be no impact to ignore these comments if you are copying the code because they are informative.

How to Run Files with Command Lines

After saving the text file, it is now the time to ask the Python to run the file. This is achieved by listing its file name and we will do it as the first argument to the Python command just like it is done at the system shell prompt. Remember, you can type a system shell command in your preferred system like an xterm window or a window command prompt to provide command-line entry. However, ensure you run it at the system prompt. Also, make sure you replace the term, 'python' with a full directory path just like we did when our PATH setting was not configured. By replacing it, the system will successfully run your program.

Additionally, as a beginner, you should not type any proceeding text in the script 1.py source file created in our last section. The texts include a system command, as well as program output. The first line must be shell command for running the source file in addition to the line.

# List, Tuples and dictionaries

## Lists

They are exactly as they sound and function pretty much the same. A list, in Python, is represented by square brackets '[]' and it can hold multiple items within it. You can store as many items or values as you like within a list and recall each component easily.

Let us look at a simple list first to see how exactly it works. For that, we have six imaginary volunteers; Joey, Chandler, Ross, Phoebe, Rachel, and Monica. Let's also assume that we have no idea of the obvious connection to these names. Time to create our first list:

friends = ["Joey", "Chandler", "Ross", "Phoebe", "Rachel", "Monica"]


And we have our list created. Since we are using string values, we will need to use quotation marks to let Python know that these are string values.

Suppose you do not know what's on the list. You do not even know how long the list is. Our target is to find out:

• The number of components within this list

• Value of individual components

To do that, we will first need to see how long the list is, and we can do just that by using the len() function. The len() function basically displays the length of characters, components or items within a variable or a list.

friends = ["Joey", "Chandler", "Ross", "Phoebe", "Rachel", "Monica"]

```
print(len(friends))
```

Output:

6

Now, we have obtained one piece of information. Moving to the next one, let us find out what is at the start of this list. To do that, we will call up the first element, and this is where the concept of index position comes in.

An index is the position of a component. Here, the first component is 'Joey' and to find out that, we will do this:

```
friends = ["Joey", "Chandler", "Ross", "Phoebe", "Rachel", "Monica"]

print(friends)
```

Here, we will use the square brackets and use the value of zero. Why zero and not one? In Python, and in quite a few languages as well, the first position is always a zero. Here, "friends" essentially tells the program to print the component with the first index position. The output, obviously, is:

Joey

Similarly, let's print the rest out accordingly!

```
friends = ["Joey", "Chandler", "Ross", "Phoebe", "Rachel", "Monica"]
```

```
print(friends)

print(friends)

print(friends)

print(friends)

print(friends)

print(friends)
```

Output:

Joey

Chandler

Ross

Phoebe

Rachel

Monica

There is another way to do this. Suppose you do not know the length of the list, and you wish to print out the last recorded entry of the same, you can do that by using the following method:

```
friends = ["Joey", "Chandler", "Ross", "Phoebe", "Rachel", "Monica"]

print(friends[-1])
```

Output:

Monica

The '-1' will always fetch you the last entry. If you use '-2' instead, it will print out the second to last entry as shown here:

friends = ["Joey", "Chandler", "Ross", "Phoebe", "Rachel", "Monica"]

print(friends[-2])

Output:

Rachel

There are other variations involved here, as well. You can call the items from a specific starting point. Using the same list above, let's assume we wish the prompt to print out the last three entries only. We can do that easily by using the starting index number of the value we wish to print. In this case, it would be the index number '3':

friends = ["Joey", "Chandler", "Ross", "Phoebe", "Rachel", "Monica"]

print(friends[3:])

 Output:

['Phoebe', 'Rachel', 'Monica']

You can also limit what you wish to see on the screen further by setting a range of index numbers. The first number, the one before the colon, represents the starting point. The number that you input after the colon is the end point. In our list of friends, we have a range from zero to five, let us narrow our results down a little:

```
friends = ["Joey", "Chandler", "Ross", "Phoebe", "Rachel", "Monica"]

print(friends[2:5])
```

Output:

```
['Ross', 'Phoebe', 'Rachel']
```

Remember, the last index number will not be printed; otherwise, the result would have also shown the last entry.

You can modify the values of a list quite easily. Suppose you wish to change the entry at index number five of the above list, and you wish to change the entry from 'Monica' to 'Geller,' this is how you would do so:

```
friends = ["Joey", "Chandler", "Ross", "Phoebe", "Rachel", "Monica"]

friends = "Geller"

print(friends)
```

Output:

```
['Joey', 'Chandler', 'Ross', 'Phoebe', 'Rachel', 'Geller']
```

It is that easy! You can use lists with loops and conditional statements to iterate over random elements and use the ones which are most suitable to the situation. Practice a little and you should soon get the hang of them.

What about if you wish to add numbers or values to the existing lists? Do we have to scroll all the way up and continue adding numbers manually? No! There are things called methods, which you can access at any given time to carry out various operations.

Here's a screen grab to show just how many options you have available to you once you press the '.' Key:

```
numbers = [99, 123, 2313, 1, 1231411, 343, 435345]
numbers.|
    m insert(self, index, object)                      list
    m append(self, object)                             list
    m clear(self)                                      list
    m copy(self)                                       list
    m count(self, object)                              list
    m extend(self, iterable)                           list
    m index(self, object, start, stop)                 list
    m pop(self, index)                                 list
    m remove(self, object)                             list
    m reverse(self)                                    list
    m sort(self, key, reverse)                         list
Ctrl+Down and Ctrl+Up will move caret down and up in the editor  Next Tip
```

We will not be talking about all of these, but we will briefly look at some basic methods that every programmer should know.

Straight away, the 'append' method is what we use to add values. Simply type in the name of the list you wish to recall, followed by ".append" to let the program know you wish to add a value. Type in the value and that is it!

The problem with using the append method is that it adds the item randomly. What if you wish to add a value to a specific index number? To do that, you will need to use the insert method.

Using an insert method, you will need to do this:

numbers = [99, 123, 2313, 1, 1231411, 343, 435345]

numbers.insert(2, 999)

print(numbers)


Output:

[99, 123, 999, 2313, 1, 1231411, 343, 435345]


The number was added right where I wanted. Remember to use an index position that is valid. If you are unsure, use the len() function to recall how many components are within a list. That should then allow you to know the index positions available.

You can also remove items from a list as well. Simply use the remove() method and input the number/value you wish to remove. Please note that if your list has more than one values that are exactly the same, this command will only remove the first instance only.

Let us assume you are presented with a list of mixed entries. There is no order that they follow. The numbers are just everywhere, disregarding the order. If you wish, you can sort the entire list to look more appealing by using the sort() method.

```
numbers = [99, 123, 2313, 1, 1231411, 99, 435345]

numbers.sort()

print(numbers)
```

Output:

[1, 99, 99, 123, 2313, 435345, 1231411]

You know, you can also have it the other way around by using the reverse() method. Try it!

To completely empty a list, you can use the clear() method. This specific method will not require you to pass any argument as a parameter. There are other methods such as pop() (which takes away the last item on the list only) that you should experiment with. Do not worry, it will not crash your system down or expose it to threats. The IDE is like a safe zone for programmers to test out various methods, programs, and scripts. Feel free and feel at ease when charting new waters.

## Tuples

As funny as the name may be, tuples are pretty much like lists. The only major difference is that these are used when you really do not wish for certain specialized values to change at all throughout the program. Once you create a tuple, it cannot be modified or changed later on.

Tuples are represented by parenthesis (). If you try and access the methods, you will no longer have access to the methods that you did when you were using lists. These are secure and used only in situations where you are certain you do not wish to change, modify, add or remove items. Normally, we will be using lists, but it is great to know we have a safe way to do things as well.

## Dictionaries

Unlike tuples and lists, dictionaries are different. To begin with, they work with "key value pairs" which sounds confusing, I know. However, let us look at what exactly a dictionary is and how we can call, create and modify the same.

To help us with the explanation, we have our imaginary friend here named James who has graciously accepted to volunteer for the exercise. We then took some information from him such as his name, email, age, the car he drives, and we ended up with this information:

Name – James

Age – 58

Email – james@domain.com

Car – Tesla T1

What we have here are called key pairs. To represent the same within a dictionary, all we need is to create one. How do we do that? Let's have a look.

```
friend = {

"name": "James",

"age": 30,

"email": "james@domain.com",

"car": "Tesla T1"

}
```

We define a dictionary using {} braces. Add each pair as shown above with a colon in the middle. Use a comma to separate items from one another. Now, you have a dictionary called 'friend' and you can access the information easily.

Now, to call up the email, we will use square brackets as shown here:

```
friend = {

"name": "James",

"age": 30,

"email": "james@domain.com",

"car": "Tesla T1"

}
```

```
print(friend["email"])
```

Output:

james@domain.com

Similarly, try recalling the other elements to try it out yourself. Once again, I remind you that Python is case sensitive. If you recall 'age' as 'Age', it will not work at all.

Suppose you wish to recall an item without knowing the key pairs within a dictionary. If you type in a key named 'dob', the program is going to return an error like this:

Traceback (most recent call last):

  File "C:/Users/Programmer/PycharmProjects/PFB/Lists2.py", line 7, in <module>

```
print(friend["dob"])
```

KeyError: 'dob'

There is a way you can check for values without the program screaming back at you with red/pink fonts. Use the .get() method instead and the program will simply say 'None,' which represents the absence of value.

You can also give any keypair, that may not have existed before, a default value as well.

```
friend = {

"name": "James",

"age": 30,

"email": "james@domain.com",

"car": "Tesla T1"

}
print(friend.get("dob", "1, 1, 1900"))
```

Output:

1, 1, 1900

Unlike tuples, you can actually add, modify or change values within a dictionary. I have already shown you how to do that with lists, but just for demonstration purposes, here's one way you can do that.

```
friend["age"] = 60

print(friend["age"])
```

Output:

60

Now, that wasn't so bad, was it? This then ends our trip to the world of lists, tuples, and dictionaries. It is vital that you pay close attention to these as you will be needing to use a few of them, if not all at once, more often than you might imagine. The more you practice and familiarize yourself with lists, tuples, and dictionaries, the easier it will be to create some incredible programs and code in efficient codes at the same time.

# Functions and Modules

## Why use modules?

Modules allow us to organize the elements and components inside our codes in an easier way, providing us with a big package of variables that are auto contained. Names that are defined on a superior level in a module file automatically will become an attribute of the object of the imported module.

Another advantage of using modules is that they let us reuse the code, using data services and linking individual files to broaden our program.

The main reason why we think that the modules are a very useful tool when it comes to programming is that they are really helpful to organize and reuse our code. This is very important when we talk about OOP (Object-Oriented Programming) since on that mode, the modularization and reusage are very popular. Since Python is a programming language oriented for that, it comes very user-friendly.

Imagine that you want to create an application or a program, more complex than what we have been doing until now. For it, you are going to need one of the previous codes to complement. Here is when you see the real benefit of the modules since you will be able to simply add one of the old codes to the complex application you want to do.

In modules, we will also have modularization. It is based on dividing our codes into several tiny pieces of codes, so that, at the moment of making the complex program or application, it won't have hundreds and hundreds of lines of codes that could be annoying and hard to read. Instead, the code will be separated into tiny files.

## How create a module on Python

Creating a module is something very easy that anyone can do, all that needs to be done is to create a file with the .py extension, then, that file will be stored on a folder of your preference; this is known as import.

In case we want to create a module of our own, you will have to do the following. We will make a program on which we will create a module that could be used later.

The module syntax is as follows:

As you could see, the syntax is really simple, since it is pretty much like creating a function. After we created it, we must be able to import it from another program, in order to do that, we will use the import statement.

## Import statement and module

Import Statement

A module is able to contain definitions of a function and even statements, which can be executable. With this, it is possible to initialize a module since they execute only when our module is on the import statement.

Modules are capable of importing other modules, that is why people use to put the import type statements at the beginning of each since with the names of our imported modules, they will locate on a space named global; function that modules have for importing.

With the help of the last example, we can manage to import the module created previously and use the functions that we defined there.

As you see in this example, we created the op variable, who takes the task of storing a string, which will specify the option that the users choose.

Then, two variables would be initialized, a and b; they will store the value of the operators we are going to use to perform the mathematical operations.

Afterward, the result variable will store the value that the function calculator returns, according to the operators and the type of operation that the users want. The function calculator comes from the module that we have imported.

When the Python interpreter finds the import statement, it imports the module, as long as it is located on the full search path. The search path is nothing but a list where all the directories that Python accesses before importing any module are located.

How to Import a Module?

For being able to import a module, we just have to follow some instructions and steps that are performed at the moment of the execution:

We look for the module through the module search path, compile to byte code, and lastly, we execute the byte-code of our module to then build an object that defines it.

How can I search for a module through Search Path?

To search for a module, our search system compounds of the concatenation of paths; these can be seen on the directory "Home" of our program. After this, the environment PYTHONPATH will be located from left to right, and that is how we will find the directory of default libraries.

Namespaces in Modules

As you know, modules are files. Python creates a module object in which all the names that we assigned in that module-file will be contained. What does that mean? This means that namespaces are just places where all the names that later become attributes are created.

What Are the Attributes?

Attributes are the names that have been assigned to a value considered of a higher level on a module file, which does not belong to

a function or class.

Calling a function in python;

A function that has been defined will only set the parameters for it and then give it its name.

At the point in time that you have set the structure for the block of code, you are going to be able to execute it by creating another function or by using Python directly in a prompt that is provided by the program.

Example

```
#! / usr/ bin/ python

#the definition for my function is going to entered in here

Def printme ( str ) :

"This will be where the string is printed"

Print str

Return;

# at this point I am going to be able to call upon the printme function
```

Printme ( "This will be where the first definition is going to go")

Printme ("This is the second definition")

Output

This will be where the first definition is going to go.

This is the second definition.

Value vs Pass by reference

When a parameter is set in Python, it has to be passed by a reference.

This means that if you are wanting to change the parameter, any change that you end up making is going to be reflected back to the function that has been called.

Example

```
#!/ usr/ bin/ python

#define your function in this space

Def nameme ( asection ) :

"This is going to be before you change anything"

Asection. Append ( [ 5, 10, 15, 20 ] );

Print "the numbers in the function I created: " , asection

Return

#here is where you are going to change your function

Asection = [ 2, 4, 6 ];

Nameme( asection ) ;
```

Print "Any number that is not in the function " , asection

Output

Numbers in the function [ 2, 4, 6, [ 5, 10, 15, 20 ] ]

Numbers not in the function [ 2, 4, 6, [ 5, 10, 15, 20 ] ]

Argument functions

There are four types of arguments that are going to be used with functions

Variable-length arguments

Required arguments

Default arguments

Keyword arguments

Required

Arguments are going to be sent through the function in the order in which the arguments are in order. It is known as a required argument.

There are various other arguments that can be used, however, the argument that you pick needs to match the definition of the function exactly or you are going to end up with an error from Python.

When you are calling upon a function, you have to ensure that it passes at least one argument or else you will end up with a error that is syntax based.

Example

#!/ usr/ bin / python

#definition of the function belongs here

Def nameme ( str )

"This will be the string that is written inside of the function"

Print str

Return ;

#this will be where the function is called upon

Nameme( )

Because no argument has been listed, you are going to end up receiving an error and having to go back and fix your code.

Keyword

Keyword arguments are going to function like when a function is called upon.

The keyword argument is going to be defined by the name of the parameter.

Thanks to this argument, you are going to be able to skip arguments or put them in a different order since the interpreter is going to be able to look at the keywords and then match it with the parameter that it needs to be placed with.

Example

#!/ usr/ bin / python

#definition of the function

Def nameme ( str ) :

"The string is going to be printed here"

Print str

Return ;

#the function can now be called upon here

Nameme ( str – "A section " )

Output

A section

You are going to be able to put your parameters where you want them without worrying about getting an error message.

Example

#! / usr/ bin / python

#definition of the function belongs here

Def printdata ( title, years of service ) :

"The data that is put into the function has to be passed through this"

Print "title: " , title

Print "years of service " , years of service

Return ;

#the function can now be called upon

Printdata ( years of service = 5, title = associate

Output

Title: associate

Years of service: 5

Defaults

Values that are not given inside of the function are going to fall back on a value that Python has deemed the default value.

Example

```
#!/ usr / bin / python

#define your function in this section

Def printdata ( title, years of service = 5) :

"The data has to be passed through this function"

Print "title : " , title

Print "years of service " , years of service

Return ;

#here is where the function will be called

Printdata ( years of service = 15, title = "associate" )

Printdata ( title = "associate" )
```

Output

Title: associate

Years of service 5

Title: associate

Years of service 15

## Functions for globals ( ) and locals ( )

These functions are going to be used so that the global and local namespaces are returned but it is going to depend the location in which they are located.

When you are working with the local ( ) function, it will give you the names that are in the function for that particular location.

A globals ( ) function is going to return the names for the function in that global location.

There is a dictionary that has all of the types for both of the functions listed. Names are going to be pulled with the keys ( ) function.

Function reload ( )

Any imported module is going to be carried out once.

Should you want to make the module be executed again, you are going to use the function reload ( ).

This function is going to reload the module that was previously imported.

## Syntax

Reload(module_name)

The module name is going to be what the module is named in the Python directory. The string name is not going to be name that is placed in this space.

Example

Reload( South )

Python Packages

There is a hierarchy when it comes to the file directory and this is going to end up defining applications that are in Python.

This package will have sub-subpackages, subpackages, and modules.

# Working with Files

The Python programming language allows us to work on two different levels when we refer to file systems and directories. One of them is through the module os, which facilitates us to work with the whole system of files and directories, at the level of the operating system itself.

The second level is the one that allows us to work with files, this is done by manipulating their reading and writing at the application level, and treating each file as an object.

In python as well as in any other language, the files are manipulated in three steps, first they are opened, then they are operated on or edited and finally they are closed.

What is a file?

A python file is a set of bytes, which are composed of a structure, and within this we find in the header, where all the data of the file is handled such as, for example, the name, size and type of file we are working with; the data is part of the body of the file, where the written content is handled by the editor and finally the end of the file, where we notify the code through this sentence that we reach the end of the file. In this way, we can describe the structure of a file.

The structure of the files is composed in the following way:

-       File header: These are the data that the file will contain (name, size, type)

-       File Data: This will be the body of the file and will have some content written by the programmer.

- End of file: This sentence is the one that will indicate that the file has reached its end.

Our file will look like this:

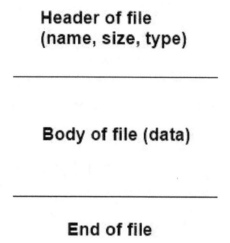

**Header of file
(name, size, type)**

_____

**Body of file (data)**

_____

**End of file**

How can I access a file?

There are two very basic ways to access a file, one is to use it as a text file, where you proceed line by line, the other is to treat it as a binary file, where you proceed byte by byte.

Now, to assign a variable a file type value, we will need to use the function open (), which will allow us to open a file.

Open() function

To open a file in Python, we have to use the open() function, since this will receive the name of the file and the way in which the file will be opened as parameters. If the file opening mode is not entered, it will open in the default way in a read-only file.

We must keep in mind that the operations to open the files are limited because it is not possible to read a file that was opened only for writing, you cannot write to a file which has been opened only for reading.

The open () function consists of two parameters:

- It is the path to the file we want to open.

- It is the mode in which we can open it.

Its syntax is as follows:

```
1    function = open("file.txt", "w")
2    function.write()
3    function.close()
```

Of which the parameters:

File: This is an argument that provides the name of the file we want to access with the open() function, this is what will be the path of our file.

The argument file is considered a fundamental argument, since it is the main one (allowing us to open the file), unlike the rest of the arguments which can be optional and have values that are already predetermined.

Mode: The access modes are those that are in charge of defining the way in which the file is going to be opened (it could be for reading, writing, editing).

There are a variety of access modes, these are:

| r | This is the default open mode. Opens the file for reading only |
|---|---|

| r+ | This mode opens the file for its reading and writing |
|----|----|
| rb | This mode opens the file for reading only in a binary format |
| w | This mode opens the file for writing only. In case the file does not exist, this mode creates it |
| w+ | This is similar to the w mode, but this allows the file to be read |
| wb | This mode is similar to the w mode, but this opens the file in a binary format |
| wb+ | This mode is similar to the wb mode, but this allows the file to be read |
| a | This mode opens a file to be added. The file starts writing from the end |
| ab | This is similar to mode a, but opens the file in a binary format |
| a+ | This mode is pretty much like the mode a, but allows us to read the file. |

In summary, we have three letters, or three main modes: r,w and a. And two submodes, + and b.

In Python, there are two types of files: Text files and plain files. It is very important to specify in which format the file will be opened to avoid any error in our code.

Read a file:

There are three ways to read a file:

1. read([n])

2. readlines()

3. readline([n])

Surely at this point, we have the question of what is meant by the letter n enclosed in parentheses and square brackets? It's very simple, the letter n is going to notify the bytes that the file is going to read and interpret.

Read method ([ ])

```
1    myfile = open("D:\\pythonfile\\mypythonfile.txt","r")
2    myfile.read(9)
```

There we could see that inside the read() there is a number 9, which will tell Python that he has to read only the first nine letters of the file

Readline(n) Method

The readline method is the one that reads a line from the file, so that the read bytes can be returned in the form of a string. The readline method is not able to read more than one line of code, even if the byte n exceeds the line quantity.

Its syntax is very similar to the syntax of the read() method.

```
1    myfile = open("D:\\pythonfile\\mypythonfile.txt","r")
2    myfile.readline()
```

Readlines(n) Method

The readlines method is the one that reads all the lines of the file, so that the read bytes can be taken up again in the form of a string. Unlike the readline method, this one is able to read all the lines.

Like the read() method and readline() its syntax are very similar:

```
1    myfile = open("D:\\pythonfile\\mypythonfile.txt","r")
2    myfile.readlines()
```

Once we have opened a file, there are many types of information (attributes) we could get to know more about our files. These attributes are:

File.name: This is an attribute that will return the name of the file.

File.mode: This is an attribute that will return the accesses with which we have opened a file.

file.closed: This is an attribute that will return a "True" if the file we were working with is closed and if the file we were working with is still open, it will return a "False".

Close() function

The close function is the method by which any type of information that has been written in the memory of our program is eliminated, in order to proceed to close the file. But that is not the only way to close a file; we can also do it when we reassign an object from one file to another file.

The syntax of the close function is as follows:

```
1    myfile.close()
2
```

What's a buffer?

We can define the buffer as a file which is given a temporary use in the ram memory; this will contain a fragment of data that composes the sequence of files in our operating system. We use buffers very often when we work with a file which we do not know the storage size.

It is important to keep in mind that, if the size of the file were to exceed the ram memory that our equipment has, its processing unit will not be able to execute the program and work correctly.

What is the size of a buffer for? The size of a buffer is the one that will indicate the available storage space while we use the file. Through the function: io.DEFAULT_BUFFER_SIZE the program will show us the size of our file in the platform in a predetermined way.

We can observe this in a clearer way:

```
1    import io
2        print("Default buffer size:"io.DEFAULT_BUFFER_SIZE)
3        file= open("Myfile.txt", mode= "r", buffering=6)
4        print(file.line_buffering)
5    file_contents=file.buffer
6    for line in file_contents
7        print(line)
```

Errors

---

In our files, we are going to find a string (of the optional type) which is going to specify the way in which we could handle the coding errors in our program.

Errors can only be used in txt mode files.

These are the following:

| Ignore_errors() | This will avoid the comments with a wrong or unknown format |
|---|---|
| Strict_errors() | This is going to generate a subclass or UnicodeError in case that any mistake or fail comes out in our code file |

Encoding

The string encoding is frequently used when we work with data storage and this is nothing more than the representation of the encoding of characters, whose system is based on bits and bytes as a representation of the same character.

This is expressed as follows:

```
1   string.encode(encoding="UTF-8", errors= "strict")
2
```

Newline

The Newline mode is the one that is going to control the functionalities of the new lines, which can be '\r', " ", none, '\n', and '\r\n'.

The newlines are universal and can be seen as a way of interpreting the text sequences of our code.

1.The end-of-line sentence in Windows: "\r\n".

2.The end-of-line sentence in Max Os: "\r".

3.The end-of-line sentence in UNIX: "\n"

 On input: If the newline is of the None type, the universal newline mode is automatically activated.

Input lines can end in "\r", "\n" or "\r\n" and are automatically translated to "\n" before being returned by our program. If their respective legal parameters when coding are met, the entry of the lines will end only by the same given string and their final line will not be translated at the time of return.

On output: If the newline is of the None type, any type of character "\n" that has been written, will be translated to a line separator which we call "os.linesep".

If the newline is of the type " " no type of translator is going to be made, and in case the newline meets any value of which are considered the legal for the code, they will be automatically translated to the string.

Example of newline reading for " ".

```
1    string.encode(mode="r", newline= " ")
2
```

Example of newline reading for none:

```
1    string.encode(mode="w", newline= "none")
2
```

Manage files through the "os" module

The "os" module allows us to perform certain operations, these will depend on an operating system (actions such as starting a process, listing files in a folder, end process and others).

There are a variety of methods with the "os" module which allow us to manage files, these are:

| | |
|---|---|
| os.makedirs() | This method of the "os" module will create a new file |
| os.path.getsize() | This method of the "os" module will show the size of a file in bytes. |
| os.remove(file_name) | This method of the "os" module will delete a file or the program |
| os.getcwd () | This method of the "os" module will show us the actual directory from where we will be working |
| os.listdir() | This method of the "os" module will list all the content of any folder of our file |

| os.rename (current_new) | This method of the "os" module will rename a file |
|---|---|
| os.path.isdir() | This method of the "os" module will transfer the parameters of the program to a folder |
| os.chdir() | This method of the "os" module will change or update the direction of any folder or directory |
| os.path.isfile() | This method of the "os" module will transform a parameter into a file. |

Xlsx files: xlsx files are those files in which you work with spreadsheets, how is this? Well, this is nothing more than working with programs like Excel. For example, if we have the windows operating system on our computer, we have the advantage that when working with this type of files, the weight of it will be much lighter than other types of files.

The xlsx type files are very useful when working with databases, statistics, calculations, numerical type data, graphics and even certain types of basic automation.

# Object Oriented Programming

When we talk about object-oriented programming, we naturally think of process-oriented programming. Process-oriented programming is to analyze the steps to solve the problem, and then use functions to implement these steps one by one when using different methods.

Object-oriented programming is to decompose the problem-solving entities into multiple objects, and the purpose of establishing objects is not to complete one by one but to describe the behavior of things in the process of solving the whole problem.

The following is an example of gobang to illustrate the difference between process-oriented and object-oriented programming.

First, use the process-oriented paradigm:

1. Start the game

2. Player 1 plays first

3. Draw the picture

4. Judges the result

5. Player 2 turn

6. Draw the picture

7. Judges the result

8. Return to Step 2

9. Output Final Results

The above steps are implemented by functions respectively, and the problem is solved using a process-oriented paradigm.

Object-oriented design solves the problem from another way of thinking. When using object-oriented thinking to realize gobang, the whole gobang game can be divided into three types of objects, as follows.

1. Black and White Parties: This represents the two players

2. Chessboard system: This is responsible for drawing pictures

3. Rule system: This is responsible for judging things such as foul, winning or losing, etc.

Among the above three-class objects, the first-class object (black and white parties) is responsible for receiving the user's input and notifying the second-class object (chessboard system) to draw pieces on the chessboard, while the third-class object (rule system) judges the chessboard.

Object-oriented programming ensures the unity of functions, thus making the code easier to maintain.

For example, if we want to add the function of chess now in a process-oriented paradigm, then a series of steps of input, judgment, and display needs to be changed. Even the loops between steps need to be adjusted on a large scale, which is very troublesome.

If object-oriented development is used, only the chessboard object needs to be changed. The chessboard object saves the chessboard scores of both black and white parties, and only needs simple backtracking, without changing the display and rules. At the same time, the calling sequence of the whole object function will not change, and its changes are only partial.

Thus, compared with process-oriented, object-oriented programming is more convenient for later code maintenance and function expansion.

## Classes and objects

In object-oriented programming, the two most important core concepts are class and object. Objects are concrete things in real life. They can be seen and touched. For example, the book you are holding is an object.

Compared with objects, classes are abstract, which is a general designation for a group of things with the same characteristics and behaviors. For example, when I was a child, my mother said to me, "Son, you should take that kind of person as an example!" The type of people here refers to a group of people who have excellent academic results and who are polite. They have the same characteristics, so they are called "same type" people.

## Relationship between Class and Object

As the saying goes, "people are grouped by category, and things are grouped by group," we collectively refer to the collection of things with similar characteristics and behaviors as categories, such as animals, airplanes, etc.

For example, the toy model can be regarded as a class and each toy as an object, thus the relationship between the toy model and the toy can be regarded as the relationship between the class and the object. Class is used to describe the common features of multiple objects and is a template for objects. An object is used to describe individuals in reality. It is an instance of a class. As can be seen, objects are created according to classes, and one class can correspond to multiple objects.

## Definition of Class

In daily life, to describe a kind of category, it is necessary to explain its characteristics as well as its uses. For example, when describing such entities as human beings, it is usually necessary to give a definition or name to such things. Human characteristics include height, weight, sex, occupation, etc. Human behaviors include running, speaking, etc. The combination of human characteristics and behaviors can completely describe human beings.

The design idea of an object-oriented program is based on this design, which includes the features and behaviors of things in classes. Among them, the characteristics of things are taken as the attributes of classes, the behaviors of things are taken as the methods of classes, and objects are an instance of classes. So to create an object, you need to define a class first. The class is composed of 3 parts.

(1) Class Name: The name of the class, whose initial letter must be uppercase, such as Person.

(2) Attribute: used to describe the characteristics of things, for example, people have the characteristics of name, age, etc.

(3) Method: Used to describe the behavior of things, for example, people have behaviors such as talking and smiling.

In Python, you can use the class keyword to declare a class with the following basic syntax format:

Class {Enter the entity here}:

# This is property of a class

# Method of class

The following is a sample code:

```
class Vehicle:

# attribute

# Method

 def drive(self):

Print ("-drivinf Automobile--")
```

In the above example, the class is used to define a class named Vehicle, in which there is a drive method. As can be seen from the example, the format of the method is the same as that of the function.

The main difference is that the method must explicitly declare a self-parameter and be located at the beginning of the parameter list. Self represents the instance of the class (object) itself, which can be used to refer to the attributes and methods of the object. The specific usage of self will be introduced later with practical application.

## Creating Objects from Classes

If a program wants to complete specific functions, classes alone are not enough but also instance objects need to be created according to classes.

In Python programs, you can use the following syntax to create an object:

Object {Enter the entity name here } = Class { Enter the name here} ()

For example, create an object Vehicle of driving class with the following sample code:

```
vehicle = driving()
```

In the above code, vehicle is a variable that can be used to access the properties and methods of the class. To add attributes to an object, you can use the following syntax.

Object {Enter entity here}. New {Enter attribute name} = Value

For example, use vehicle to add the color attribute to an object of driving class.

The sample code is as follows:

vehicle.color = "black"

Next, a complete case is used to demonstrate how to create objects, add attributes and call methods. Look at it and clear all your doubts.

Example Spo

```
# Define Class

class Football:

# kick

def kick(goal):

print ("You scored ..." )

# Foul

def foul(self):

print ("You cheated" )

# creates an object and saves its reference with the variable BMW

Barcelona = Football()
```

```
# Add Attribute Representing Color

Barcelona.color = "blue"

# Call Method

Barcelona.goal()

Barcelona.foul()

# Access Attributes

print(Barcelona.color)
```

In Example, a Football class is defined, two methods kick and foul is defined in the class, then an object Barcelona of football class is created, color attribute is dynamically added and assigned to "blue", then goal () and foul () methods are called in turn, and the value of color attribute is printed out.

# Structural Methods and Destructural Methods

In Python programs, two special methods are provided: __init__() and __del (), which are respectively used to initialize the properties of the object and release the resources occupied by the class.

# Construction method

In the previous example defining classes, we dynamically added the color attribute to the objects referenced by Barcelona. Just imagine, if you create another Football class object, you need to add attributes in the form of "object name. attribute name". For each object created, you need to add attributes once, which is very troublesome.

To solve this problem, attributes can be set when creating an object. Python provides a construction method with a fixed name of_init_(two underscores begin and two underscores end). When creating an instance of a class, the system will automatically call the constructor to initialize the class.

To make everyone better understand, the following is a case to demonstrate how to use the construction method for initialization.

Example: uses the construction method. py

# Define Class

class Football:

# construction method

def__init__(kick):

Color = "blue"

# Foul

```python
def foul(self):

print ("%s Barcelona color is " (self.color))

# creates an object and saves its reference with the variable car

football = Football()

football.foul()
```

In the example, lines 4-5 re-implemented the_init__() method, adding the color attribute to the Football class and assigning it a value of "blue", and accessing the value of the color attribute in the foul method.

No matter how many Football objects are created, the initial value of the color attribute is "blue" by default. If you want to modify the default value of the property after the object is created, you can set the value of the property by passing parameters in the construction method.

The following is a case to demonstrate how to use the construction method with parameters.

Example: uses the parametric construction method. py

```python
# Define Class

class Football:

# construction method

def___init__(kick):

Color = "blue"

# Foul
```

```python
def foul(self):

print ("%s Barcelona color is " (self.color))

# creates an object and saves its reference with the variable car

football = Football()

football.foul()

# creates an object and saves its reference with the variable bmw

realmadrid = color ("white")

realmadrid.color()
```

In Example, lines 4 to 5 customize the construction method with parameters, and assign the value of the parameters to the color attribute, ensuring that the value of the color attribute changes with the value received by the parameters, and then still access the value of the color attribute in the toot method.

## Destructor Methods

Earlier, we introduced the___init___() method. When an object is created, the Python interpreter will call the___init___() method by default. When deleting an object to release the resources occupied by the class, the Python interpreter calls another method by default, which is the___del___() method.

Next, a case is used to demonstrate how to use a destructor to release the occupied resources.

example: using destructor. py

```
# Define Class

class Football

 def___init___(team, color, name):

 team.name = name

 team.color = color

 def___del___(team):

 print("_____del_____")

Realmadrid = team ("white", 1)
```

In Example, a class named Person is defined, the initial values of color and team are set in the___init___() method, a print statement is added in the ___del___() method, and then an object of the Person class is created using a custom construction method.

When the program ends, the memory space it occupies will be released.

So, can we release the space manually? Yes, Del statement can be used to delete an object and release the resources it occupies.

Add the following code at the end of Example:

del realmadrid

print("_____1_____")

As you can observe from the results, the program outputs "del" before "1". This is because Python has an automatic garbage collection mechanism. When the Python program ends, the Python interpreter detects whether there is currently any memory space to be freed. If there is a del statement, it will be automatically deleted; if the del statement has been manually called, it will not be automatically deleted.

# Conclusion

We have come a long way. In this guide, I explained to you the basics of Python language. Learning to program is like learning another language. It takes a lot of patience, study, application, method, passion and above all perseverance.

What I can suggest is to do as much practice as possible by starting to rewrite the hundreds of examples you find in this guide.

Try to memorize them and when you write the code, say it to yourself, in your mind (open bracket, close round brackets and so on). In the beginning, this helped me a lot to memorize better the various steps needed to write a program even if simple.

It is important not to feel like heroes when a program works but above all you should not be depressed when you cannot find a solution to your programming problems. The network is full of sites and blogs where you can always find a solution.

In this 21st century, we can't forget about the importance of web area and happily, Python is surprisingly flexible in developing business enterprise well-known web solutions. The web applications demanding more speed and electricity can be executed with Python. All types of records driven internet applications can be advanced in Python with maximum power and potential.

Python is a dynamic language and supports particular programming patterns which include object- oriented, aspect-oriented, purposeful and imperative. One of the quality capabilities of the language is natural and better memory management.

Primarily employed like a scripting language, Python gives a high-quality degree of functionality. While it may be used as a standalone application, you can also integrate third birthday party gear and personalize its functionality.

Python is thought for its smooth readability. The center philosophies of the language are simple - simplicity over complexity; beauty over ugliness, express over implicit and other similar aphorisms. The most critical view of the language is "Readability Counts," which means that the syntaxes and codes written the use of Python are clean and neat.

The programming language has a huge library that helps programmers. Python additionally has an open source version referred to as the CPython programming platform. It has a massive community of builders who continuously paintings to upgrade features.

Owing to the ease of handling, Python is a "programmer's language". Moreover, studying the language is very simple. One of the most abundant blessings of Python, except clean and without problems readable codes, is the velocity with which you could code.

Programmers can pass on rapid tune because a couple of levels that aren't necessary can be skipped. Another advantage is that programmers get numerous assist from the Python open source developer community.

The portability characteristic of Python is another certainly one of its primary strengths. Not only can Python run on multiple platforms, however also programmers simplest want to write down a single application to work on all operating systems. It is a pretty adaptable language.

Learning Python is not a tough project, even for beginners. So, take the soar and master Python.